HOW TO GET RICH IN THE CALIFORNIA GOLD RUSH

AN ADVENTURER'S GUIDE
TO THE
FABULOUS RICHES DISCOVERED IN 1848

INCLUDES

PRACTICAL ADVICE REGARDING THE TERRIBLE DANGERS
OF LIVING IN A FRONTIER LAND;

CONTAINS

SCENES AND INCIDENTS OF A PROSPECTOR'S VOYAGE
(YOURS TRULY, T. HARTLEY) THROUGH THE GOLD FIELDS

WITH

MAPS OF THE ROUTES TO THOSE LANDS

AND

SKETCHES OF THE EXOTIC AND OCCASIONALLY FAMOUS CHARACTERS
ENCOUNTERED ALONG THE WAY;

NOT TO MENTION

ESSENTIAL INFORMATION REGARDING EQUIPMENT
AND SUPPLIES NEEDED TO DIG FOR GOLD

Thomas Hartley

Tod Olson • Illustrations by Scott Allred • Afterword by Marc Aronson

NATIONAL GEOGRAPHIC

WASHINGTON, D.C.

EDITOR'S NOTE: This extraordinary guide to the California gold rush is the work of the adventurer, prospector, and aspiring writer Thomas Hartley. (I swear.) Mr. Hartley recorded the account of his travels between the years of 1849 and 1851, hoping it would be published and provide useful advice to thousands of eager gold hunters. He was frustrated in this hope but apparently never gave up on his dream of seeing his journal in print. I am pleased to finally bring this exciting relic from a time of great enterprise and adventure to the public's attention.

Certain naysayers, killjoys, and garden-variety skeptics may question the authenticity of such a remarkable manuscript. I can only say in response: You do believe everything you read, don't you?

I can, however, verify the general accuracy of Mr. Hartley's account. His descriptions of the tools used in the diggings, the conditions in the mines and the towns, and general incidents are among the most reliable records of the time period. Further, his meticulous financial records—of money made and lost, of debts incurred, of (occasional!) windfall profits—give the reader an extraordinary eye-level view of what life in the gold fields must really have been like. Many of the characters he sketched along the way did in fact exist outside the imaginations of the people who made this book. If that explanation fails to satisfy the skeptic's curiosity, you may turn to my afterword at the back of the book, where the mystery of Mr. Hartley is considered (though I cannot promise you resolved) in more detail.

—MARC ARONSON

PLEASE NOTE: Neither the particulars of Mr. Hartley's journey nor, in fact, the existence of Mr. Hartley himself can be verified by independent means. The reader will simply have to enjoy the book for the lively slice of history contained within and, of course, for the fun of it all.

BEFORE WE BEGIN

IT MUST FIRST BE NOTED that travel to the gold regions should not be taken lightly. Anyone setting out for California will be leaving the luxuries of civilized life behind. Feather beds, hansom carriages, and fine china are not to be expected in the wild lands of the West. But then, the road to riches is rarely an easy one. It is hoped that this guide will serve to limit the dangers and hardships experienced along the way and so lead the prospector as gently as possible to his pot of gold. In this spirit, we shall begin with a portrait of a well-prepared voyager. . .

Balance scale, for weighing your fortune

Shovel (do not skimp on quality)

Knives (not recommended for use against grizzly bears)

Pots & pans (those who do not yet know how to cook will learn fast)

Pickaxe, for breaking rocks and one's back

Pistol (do not under any circumstances use against your fellow miners, unless one of them attempts to steal your claim)

CONTENTS

MATTERS TO BE ADDRESSED WITHIN THE PAGES OF
THIS BOOK INCLUDE, BUT ARE NOT LIMITED TO...

6 GOLD FEVER, in which the Author and all the nation
are stricken by the glorious disease

8 HOME SWEET HOME, including six reasons to leave it
behind and get your backside to the gold fields as quick as a jackrabbit

10 GETTING THERE BY LAND, featuring several good reasons
for rejecting the very long, extensive, and interminable overland route

12 GETTING THERE BY SEA, in which I and my companions
set out for California; featuring a helpful map of the route

14 SAN FRANCISCO, JULY 30, 1849, in which I paint
with considerable skill the great city as I found it

16 GETTING TO THE DIGGINGS, including a useful guide
to the tools of your trade

18 SWEET SUCCESS!, in which honest labor earns our company of
adventuring prospectors their first taste of gold

20 SEEING THE ELEPHANT, an honest account of the pleasures of
blistered fingers, aching backs, rotting teeth, scurvy, dysentery, and the pox

22 GETTING ALONG, wherein a new miner learns to handle
the rest of humanity, most of which is represented in the mines

24 INTO THE WILDERNESS, in which we follow Stoddard
into the mountains in search of the gold lake

26 LAKE OF EMPTY DREAMS, in which Stoddard is
unmasked and subjected to frontier justice

28 THE RECKONING, in a moment of sober reflection on our fortunes, we decide to part ways

30 RICH BAR, NOVEMBER 1849, wherein I show with my paintbrush the great waterworks behind my first fortune in gold.

32 A LESSON LEARNED, being a warning for young and wealthy miners set loose in the wicked city

34 ALL THAT GLITTERS IS NOT GOLD, in which faith and self-reliance begin their return

36 MAN WITH A PLAN, relating a tearful reunion between two friends and the beginnings of a profitable business

38 MARYSVILLE, SEPTEMBER 1850, being a panoramic view of our grand new enterprise

40 TALE OF WOE, in which Lansford is discovered in dire condition and recounts his grim adventures since we parted

42 HOME SWEET HOME, AGAIN, on returning with your head held high

44 THOMAS HARTLEY'S GOLD RUSH, an Afterword by Marc Aronson

45 LIST OF ILLUSTRATIONS and suggestions for FURTHER READING

46 ENCYCLOPEDIA OF THE GOLD RUSH, in which unusual words are defined and additional information is offered about historical figures and places mentioned in the text.

GOLD FEVER

IN WHICH THE AUTHOR AND ALL THE NATION ARE STRICKEN BY THE GLORIOUS DISEASE

Here's John Sutter, who owned the land where the first strike was made. You would think him lucky, but already the hordes have overrun his land and taken the gold for themselves.

The Author (henceforward plainly referred to as "I") first heard of the astounding discoveries in December 1848. I was milking in the barn when friend and fellow adventurer Jim Bartlett came to announce it. He fairly screamed the news at me, putting a fright into the cattle. With just a shovel and a pan, men in California were picking nuggets worth $50 a day out of streambeds. One newspaper reported finds of $700 a day! In a matter of weeks all talk in Massachusetts and elsewhere was of GOLD, how much and how to get it and how to spend it once you've got it. In my village alone, dozens of people prepared to leave for California. I could think of nothing else.

$3,910 worth of the enchanting treasure was displayed at the U.S. Treasury. (In reality, only 15 pounds — but a man must dream a little.)

AIR LINE, *through by daylight Passage $50. Each Passenger must provide a boy to hold his hair on.*

Augustus, dont you wish we were down, and not up.
Yes - for I begin to feel air sick - Oh dear! Oh dear!

Passengers landed by Parachutes

Stand from under.

LITH. & PUB. BY N. CURRIER,

Do not laugh. The inventor Rufus Porter advertises an "aerial locomotive" to transport gold seekers for just $50. The device boasts a steam engine and is said to be arrowproof. Two hundred people signed up, but the monstrosity never made it off the ground.

rk Herald

THE RUSH TO CALIFORNIA

INCIDENTS ON THE INCREASE—SCENES IN NEW YORK JANUARY 22, 1849. We will endeavor to give some idea of the revolution that is going on in our midst, caused by the thirst after gold. It is an epidemic, and now rages with a violence that threatens to depopulate New York.

My hair!! how the wind blow

ROCKET LINE.

through in advance of the Telegraph
Passengers not found, (if lost.)

Hold on there I've paid my passage and I aint aboard.

Bill, I'm afraid we cant get aboard.

Passage $125 and found (if lost.)

I'm bound to go anyhow

As far as I know, no one has yet attempted to swim to California.

THE WAY THEY GO TO CALIFORNIA.

152 NASSAU ST. COR. OF SPRUCE

As far as I know, no one has yet attempted to swim to California.

7

HOME SWEET HOME

INCLUDING SIX REASONS TO LEAVE IT BEHIND AND GET YOUR BACKSIDE TO THE GOLD FIELDS AS QUICK AS A JACKRABBIT

I announced my intentions quickly: I was to leave for California as soon as I could afford the journey. Every adventurous gold seeker encounters resistance from friends and family, and that was no less true of myself. My sketches will acquaint the reader with the individuals opposed and those in favor.

Yours Truly, Tom Hartley

Opposed

"Who will help your father with the cows?"

My mother, Jane Hartley

My sweetheart, Eva Braintree

"A darn fool notion if I've ever heard one."

"You shall get yourself killed, Tom Hartley."

My father, Elijah Hartley

In Favor

"Oh, I guess I'll go. But isn't there gold in Connecticut? Connecticut is considerably closer than California."

My friend, Lansford Jennings

"How will we spend the first million, Tom?"

My friend, Jim Bartlett

O' New England

It is widely agreed in these parts that farming is an honorable pursuit, for it requires long hours of backbreaking labor with little chance that wealth or comfort will ever corrupt one's soul.

I calculated this comparison to show to my father.

After studying it, he grew exceedingly quiet during our family debates.

At home last year

Income
(from sale of milk, beef, butter, etc.): $480

Expenses
(tools, feed, cloth, food, etc.): $620

Net: −$140

In the gold fields

At least $16 a day × 300 days = $4,800 !!!*

*The careful reader will note with some wariness that I failed to calculate expenses in California.

ANYONE PLANNING TO LEAVE FRIENDS AND FAMILY BEHIND WILL NEED TO EXPRESS THEIR REASONS WISELY AND FORCEFULLY TO THEIR LOVED ONES. THESE WERE MY OWN:

1. LEARN THE WAYS OF THE WORLD. (I WAS, AFTER ALL, JUST 17.)

2. BECOME RICH.

3. SETTLE OUR FAMILY DEBT OF $2,200.

4. **BECOME RICH!**

5. BUY A MODEST HOME FOR EVA AND MYSELF.

6. **BECOME RICH!**

GETTING THERE BY LAND

FEATURING SEVERAL GOOD REASONS FOR REJECTING THE VERY LONG, EXTENSIVE, AND INTERMINABLE OVERLAND ROUTE

WHAT TO CARRY

(MY GRATITUDE TO MR. JOSEPH E. WARE, WHO INCLUDED THIS LIST IN HIS OWN FINE GUIDE TO CALIFORNIA.)

4 YOKE OXEN	$200.00
1 DONKEY	50.00
1 WAGON	100.00
3 RIFLES	60.00
LEAD, 30 LBS.	1.20
POWDER, 25 LBS.	5.50
FLOUR, 1,080 LBS.	20.00
BACON, 600 LBS.	30.00
COFFEE, 100 LBS.	8.00
TEA, 5 LBS.	2.75
SUGAR, 150 LBS.	7.00
RICE, 75 LBS.	3.75
DRIED FRUIT, 50 LBS.	3.00
SALT, PEPPER, &C., 50 LBS.	3.00
LARD, 50 LBS.	2.50
SALERATUS BISCUITS, 10 LBS	1.00
COOKING UTENSILS, 30 LBS.	4.00
MINING TOOLS, 36 LBS.	12.00
TENT, 30 LBS.	5.00
BEDDING, 45 LBS.	22.50
MATCHES	1.00
CANDLES AND SOAP	5.30
PRIVATE BAGGAGE, 150 LBS.	
TOTAL .... 2,516 LBS.	$547.50

While my family argued, Jim, Lansford, and I considered the problem of gold seekers everywhere: We lived here (Massachusetts); the gold lived there (California). It cost money to get there from here, and we had exactly $25.50 among us. We first considered the overland voyage I've mapped here for the reader. This route was favored by Lansford as it is cheaper and does not involve the possibility of drowning or being eaten by sea monsters. It is, however, longer than the sea voyage. And, as Jim pointed out, "That gold is like Eva; it ain't just going to set there and wait for you, Tom."

Mr. J. M. Hutchings
made the visual account of the land voyage at right; the map is mine.
(Mr. Hutchings, incidentally, made and lost several fortunes in the mines before deciding that publishing might afford him a more stable income.)

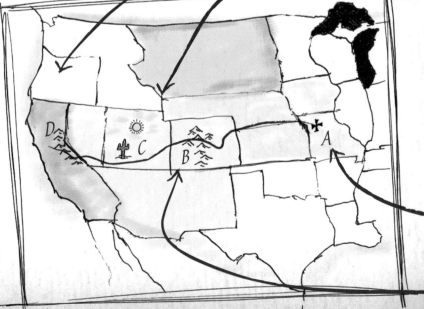

D) *The final obstacle*. Narrow mountain passes, huge boulders, and ice-cold stream crossings. In 1846, a party led by the Donner family had to winter in the mountains here. Some say they ate the dead in order to survive. Lansford insists there are <u>no</u> choice cuts of meat on his bones.

C) *Enjoy the desert scenery*: barren ground, poison water holes, animal carcasses.

B) *Onto the Rockies*: Keep your wagon <u>on</u> the trail.

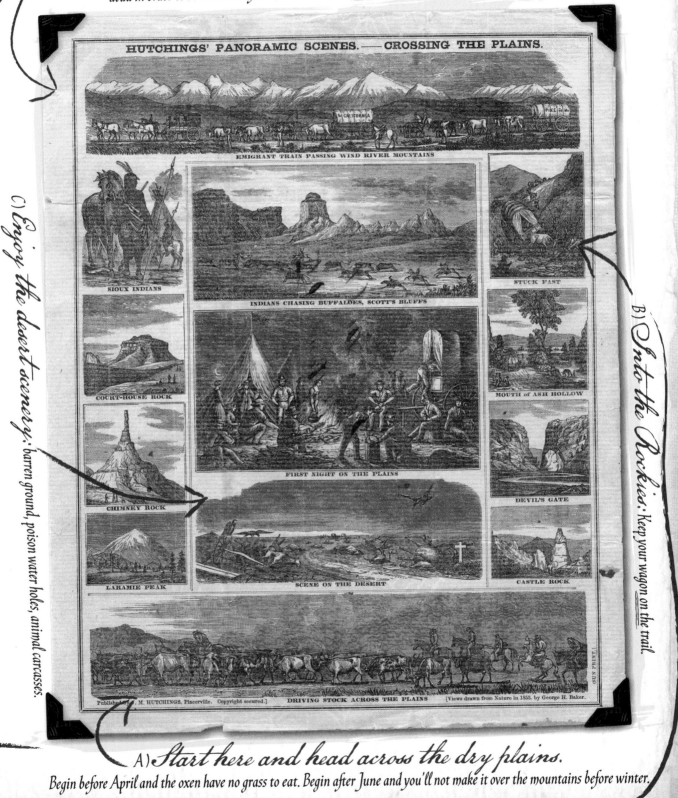

HUTCHINGS' PANORAMIC SCENES. —— CROSSING THE PLAINS.

EMIGRANT TRAIN PASSING WIND RIVER MOUNTAINS

SIOUX INDIANS

INDIANS CHASING BUFFALOES, SCOTT'S BLUFFS

STUCK FAST

COURT-HOUSE ROCK

MOUTH of ASH HOLLOW

CHIMNEY ROCK

FIRST NIGHT ON THE PLAINS

DEVIL'S GATE

LARAMIE PEAK

SCENE ON THE DESERT

CASTLE ROCK

Published by J. M. HUTCHINGS, Placerville. Copyright secured.] DRIVING STOCK ACROSS THE PLAINS [Views drawn from Nature in 1853, by George H. Baker.

A) *Start here and head across the dry plains.*
Begin before April and the oxen have no grass to eat. Begin after June and you'll not make it over the mountains before winter.

GETTING THERE BY SEA

IN WHICH I AND MY COMPANIONS SET OUT FOR CALIFORNIA

I n March it was settled. We would go by sea, with thanks to Jim's uncle in Boston. The man has made many thousands of dollars trading in whale oil, and he thought it a good investment to spend one or two on us. The arrangement was as follows. We must pay him one-quarter our earnings in the gold fields up to $1,000 each. In return he would secure for us second-class passage to Panama ($100 ea.) and give us each $500 in addition for the rest of the passage and supplies. As for my family and Eva, the growing possibility of sudden wealth softened their concern for my safety. And so, with tearful goodbyes, we set off for Springfield by wagon and from there to Boston by train.

Avoid steerage at all costs. We found this ticket in our compartment en route from Panama along with every other manner of waste, human and otherwise. I can only hope its owner had a more comfortable journey than ours. We were 160 people crowded into a single room without a window.

The bearer Mr. _____ _____ is entitled to a passage on board the SHIP HUMBOLT from this to Saint Francisco California for which I have received the amount due for passage, in the Steerage
Panama April 20; 1849

Horses were overmatched by the Panamanian jungle. We traveled by bungos (dugout canoes) for an astonishing $40, and the robbers who call themselves boat captains demanded more for cargo space. I had no choice but to abandon my gold-washing machine on the banks.

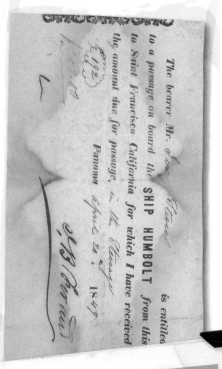

CROSSING THE ISTHMUS.

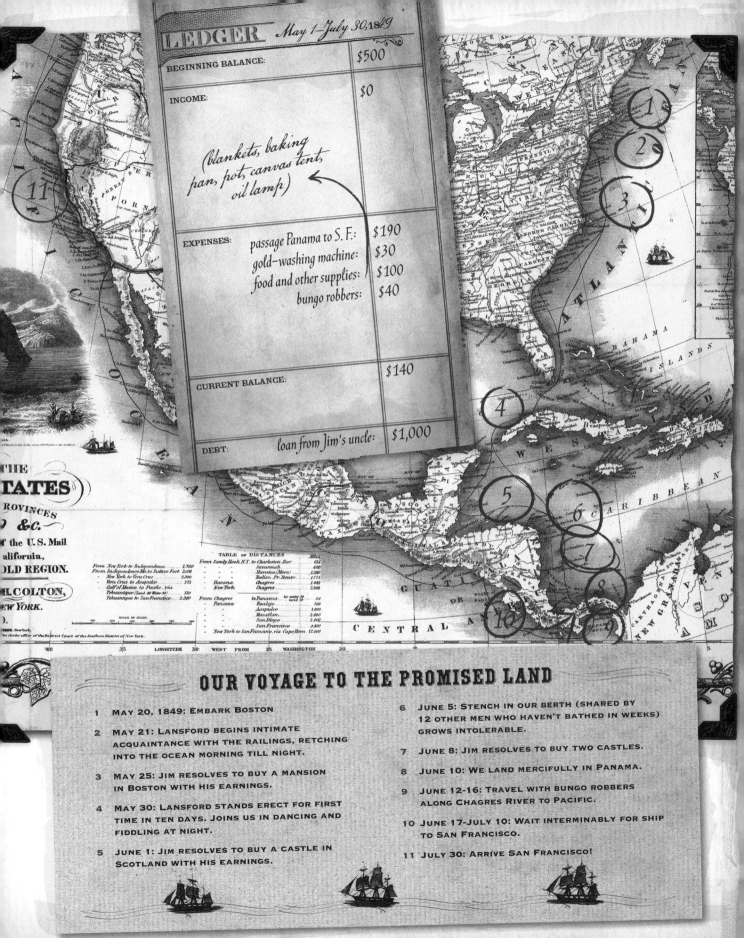

LEDGER
May 1–July 30, 1849

BEGINNING BALANCE:	$500
INCOME:	$0
EXPENSES:	
passage Panama to S.F.:	$190
gold-washing machine:	$30
food and other supplies:	$100
bungo robbers:	$40
CURRENT BALANCE:	$140
DEBT: *loan from Jim's uncle:*	$1,000

(blankets, baking pan, pot, canvas tent, oil lamp)

OUR VOYAGE TO THE PROMISED LAND

1 MAY 20, 1849: EMBARK BOSTON

2 MAY 21: LANSFORD BEGINS INTIMATE ACQUAINTANCE WITH THE RAILINGS, RETCHING INTO THE OCEAN MORNING TILL NIGHT.

3 MAY 25: JIM RESOLVES TO BUY A MANSION IN BOSTON WITH HIS EARNINGS.

4 MAY 30: LANSFORD STANDS ERECT FOR FIRST TIME IN TEN DAYS. JOINS US IN DANCING AND FIDDLING AT NIGHT.

5 JUNE 1: JIM RESOLVES TO BUY A CASTLE IN SCOTLAND WITH HIS EARNINGS.

6 JUNE 5: STENCH IN OUR BERTH (SHARED BY 12 OTHER MEN WHO HAVEN'T BATHED IN WEEKS) GROWS INTOLERABLE.

7 JUNE 8: JIM RESOLVES TO BUY TWO CASTLES.

8 JUNE 10: WE LAND MERCIFULLY IN PANAMA.

9 JUNE 12-16: TRAVEL WITH BUNGO ROBBERS ALONG CHAGRES RIVER TO PACIFIC.

10 JUNE 17-JULY 10: WAIT INTERMINABLY FOR SHIP TO SAN FRANCISCO.

11 JULY 30: ARRIVE SAN FRANCISCO!

San Francisco,
July 30, 1849

We met attorney William Daingerfield near the docks. "Gold is measured here by bushels and shovelfuls," he told us. Jim could not restrain himself. He threw his arms around the man in joy.

This man cornered us just as we got off the boat and offered me three ounces in gold ($54) for my boots, which cost $3 in Massachusetts! Luckily I had an extra pair.

A man I know even today only as Stoddard stands here. In a secretive whisper, he offered us a map showing the richest parts of the gold fields for just three ounces in gold. Having just acquired that much, we eagerly agreed.

Tents and hastily built shanties adorn the hills overlooking San Francisco. The city grew from 800 people to 15,000 in just a year, and most of the newcomers had little choice but to rough it.

Ships, abandoned by their gold–hungry crews, have been turned into hotels or gambling houses.

Do not be shocked to see crates of food and other supplies rotting at the docks. The city lacks storage.

OUTFITTERS

SALOON

BANK

GREENE OUTFITTER

MARKET

HOTEL

HOTEL

MAPS

FEED

SMITH

JANES

LEDGER

July 30, 18 49

BEGINNING BALANCE:		$140
INCOME:	*(thank heaven for the boots)*	$54
EXPENSES:	passage ship to shore:	$5
	dinner:	$8
	room:	$10
	Stoddard's map:	$54
CURRENT BALANCE: *We must away to the gold fields before we are broke.*		$117*
DEBT:	loan from Jim's uncle:	$1,000

GETTING TO THE DIGGINGS

INCLUDING A USEFUL GUIDE TO THE TOOLS OF YOUR TRADE

With the stranger

Stoddard's map to guide us,
we made our way to the diggings.

- - - - - BY BOAT (and sheer luck)

———— BY DONKEY

Anyone who thinks the journey has ended when they reach San Francisco is sorely mistaken. The biggest adventure is yet to come. We purchased passage to Sacramento on a sailing ship so overloaded with freight that Lansford asked of the captain if we couldn't find our way to the river bottom for a bit cheaper than $16. The captain only mumbled that he would be just as happy to fill our place with a few barrels of flour, for which he would make just as much.

At Jim's urging we boarded anyway and arrived (mostly) dry at Sacramento in five days. We supplied ourselves for the gold fields at no small cost, our final purchase being a donkey. We named her Ernestine after Lansford's mother, for the two bore a distinct resemblance to each other. With our newest partner leading the way, we set off for the gold fields.

$ $ $ $ $ $ $ $ $

BRING WHAT YOU CAN FROM HOME. THERE YOU CAN BUY WITH **$1** WHAT WILL COST **$10** IN SACRAMENTO AND **$20** IN THE DIGGINGS.

$ $ $ $ $ $ $ $ $

Ernestine: $125*

Remember this location! (future home of Marysville)

LEDGER (July 31, – Aug. 20, 1849)

BEGINNING BALANCE:	$117
INCOME:	$0
EXPENSES: (1/3 food, supplies, donkey):	$114.17*

*Ernestine's owner asked for $125 but took $50 (all we could pay) and a promise to pay him $150 more from our earnings in the gold fields. My share of the debt comes to $50, a mere three ounces of gold.

CURRENT BALANCE:	$2.83
DEBT: $150 for Ernestine (1/3 share):	$50
loan from Jim's uncle:	$1,000

Five pounds butter: $1.50/pound

In addition: boiled beef, salt pork, potatoes (protects against scurvy), dried apples (guaranteed to keep the bowels open)

oil lamp

blankets

baking pan

pails: $5 ea.

barrels flour: $14/barrel

2 shovels: $8 ea.

40 pounds sugar: 18 cents/pound

pot

10 pounds coffee: 18 cents/pound

canvas tent

tin pans for washing pay dirt: $5 ea. (50 cents at home)

1 ax: $10

pickaxes: $10 ea. ($1 at home)

SWEET SUCCESS!

IN WHICH HONEST LABOR EARNS OUR COMPANY OF ADVENTURING PROSPECTORS THEIR FIRST TASTE OF GOLD

At long last we arrived. Strangely, we found a hundred or more prospectors already working the "secret location" Mr. Stoddard had sold us. Undaunted, we found a promising stretch of river bed, rolled up our sleeves, and began to work.

And such sweet work it was those first days. Every hopeful prospector recalls the first golden nugget pulled from a pan of earth with his own hands. I, for one, thought that I would never look at a handful of common dirt in the same way. The very ground we trampled would from that day forward be the home of hidden treasure, a sign of the endless possibility to be found in the most unlikely places.

My first nugget!

But the reader desires practical advice, not such flights of fancy. And so, I present a guide, drawn from our experience in the diggings. . .

HOW TO MINE FOR GOLD

COMPRISING INDISPENSABLE ADVICE FOR THE NOVICE PROSPECTOR

FINDING A CLAIM

1. Look for sandbars in the river. As the water carries gold downstream, the heavy particles of metal catch against obstacles.

2. The best claims have milky-white quartz rock, brick-red soil, or slate rock. These materials seem to attract the gold.

3. Once you've found a claim, DEFEND IT WITH YOUR LIFE.

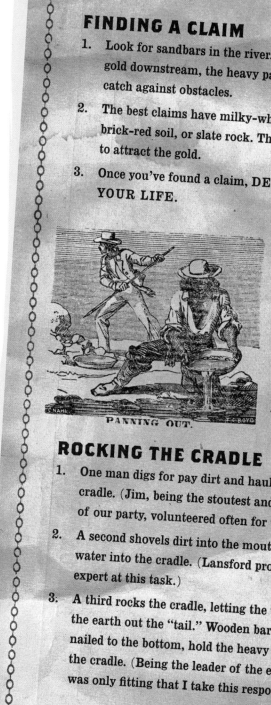

PANNING OUT.

PANNING

1. Fill a pan with dirt and water.

2. Swirl the water in the pan and let it run out. Gold is heavier than dirt and will stay behind while all else washes out.

3. Repeat until only pebbles and flakes of gold are left.

4. Carefully discard the pebbles and collect the rest.

ROCKING THE CRADLE

1. One man digs for pay dirt and hauls it to the cradle. (Jim, being the stoutest and most eager of our party, volunteered often for this duty.)

2. A second shovels dirt into the mouth, then pours water into the cradle. (Lansford proved to be an expert at this task.)

3. A third rocks the cradle, letting the water carry the earth out the "tail." Wooden bars, or "riffles" nailed to the bottom, hold the heavy gold inside the cradle. (Being the leader of the expedition it was only fitting that I take this responsibility.)

ROCKING THE CRADLE.

The Chinese travel 6,000 miles by boat to California and are experts at operating a cradle singlehandedly.

SEEING THE ELEPHANT

AN HONEST ACCOUNT OF THE PLEASURES OF BLISTERED FINGERS, ACHING BACKS, ROTTING TEETH, SCURVY, DYSENTERY, AND THE POX

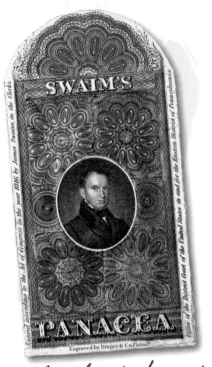

In all fairness to the novice miner, it must be said that the thrill of finding that first lump of gold does not describe the full range of emotion one experiences in the diggings. In addition to elation, there is frustration, exhaustion, disillusionment, loneliness, disappointment, and regret. And we mustn't forget pain. Quite a bit of pain.

For six weeks, our determined party worked dawn till dusk and made perhaps two ounces a day among us. Jim had bloody and blistered fingers to show for his efforts. Lansford, who vomited his way through our ocean voyage, now suffered an equivalent misery at the other end of his digestive tract. And I lay abed with the scurvy.

This, reader, is what is known in the diggings as "seeing the elephant."

Avoid popular remedies such as Swaim's Panacea. Its proprietor claims that it cures cancer, scrofula, rheumatism, gout, hepatitis, and in fact "all disorders arising from a contaminated or impure state of the blood." Its active ingredients? Sarsaparilla, wintergreen, and, of course, alcohol.

You will see by the names given to some of the diggings what the miners think of their chosen occupation:

I have seen many wonders in California, but no elephants in the flesh. The beast is merely a poetic way to speak of the hardship awaiting us all in the land of plenty.

DISEASES & THEIR REPUTED CURES:

DISEASE	SYMPTOMS	CURE
SCURVY	SWOLLEN LEGS, STIFF AND PAINFUL JOINTS, BLEEDING GUMS, DEATH	RAW POTATOES, FRESH FRUIT, MUSTARD PLASTER
DYSENTERY	FEVER, DIARRHEA, DEATH	RICE THREE TIMES A DAY, OAK BARK TEA, PEPPERMINT, AND MUSTARD PLASTER
CHOLERA	FEVER, DIARRHEA, VOMITING, DEATH	MUSTARD PLASTER, DALLY'S AND CONNELL'S MAGIC PAIN EXTRACTOR

LEDGER *Aug. 20 – Sept. 30, 1849*	
BEGINNING BALANCE:	$2.83
INCOME: 2 oz. gold/day (1/3 share):	$384
EXPENSES: food, cradle, rifle, etc (1/3 share):	$320
On the third day out from Sacramento, our beloved Ernestine went swimming with our flour and other provisions on her back.	
CURRENT BALANCE:	$66.83
DEBT: $150 for Ernestine (1/3 share):	$50
loan from Jim's uncle:	$1,000
NOTE:	

GETTING ALONG

WHEREIN A NEW MINER LEARNS TO HANDLE THE REST OF HUMANITY, MOST OF WHICH IS REPRESENTED IN THE MINES

*G*entle souls, softened by life in the East, will find that natural hazards are not the only obstacles to great riches in California. Hazards of the human variety are just as vexing. In addition to technical knowledge, the new miner must quickly acquire a hardy tolerance for the full range of humanity. The diggings are no place for prim minds easily startled, for in the gold fields is the whole world: saints and sinners, schemers and their marks, drinking men and tea sippers, gamblers and misers, freed slaves, cunning Chinamen, Frenchmen, Germans, Chileans, and adventurers from any nation you might name, all hungry for gold.

I've met colored men who were brought here to find gold for their masters and dug up enough to buy their own freedom.

The freedman seeks his future and his fortune in the riverbed.

Mr. Remington

FOR EVERY HONEST MINER

THERE IS A SCOUNDREL EAGER TO RELIEVE THE FORMER OF HIS GOLD. TO WARD OFF THE SCOUNDRELS, YOU MAY FIND IT NECESSARY TO MAKE AN ALLIANCE WITH MR. COLT OR MR. REMINGTON.

Mr. Colt

The Indians who once had this land to themselves, now man Long Toms to get back a few grains of gold.

Should you encounter a Chinaman, do not look upon him with suspicion. Chinese merchants bring rice, grain, sugar, dried fruit, and tea to sell. Those who choose to prospect work the mines with great industry and skill.

Nothing makes a man madder than to see a snaking hand thieving what he dug up himself — but you can't always tell who is the finder and who the varmint — and fists settle the matter.

CALIFORNIA GOLD DIGGERS.
Mining Operations on the Western shore of the Sacramento River

Do not imagine you will mine alone. The whole world is here, beside you.

INTO THE WILDERNESS

IN WHICH WE FOLLOW STODDARD INTO THE MOUNTAINS IN SEARCH OF THE GOLD LAKE

Jim, Lansford, and I looked much like these miners, dreams buried under a mountain of dirt.

By the end of September, disappointment began to strain the bonds of friendship. As our supplies from Sacramento ran out, expenses exceeded our earnings. We watched three parties strike it rich not 100 yards from our diggings, yet we still pulled out less than an ounce a day for each of us. Jim and I argued over where to dig. Lansford spoke of going home. Ernestine fashioned a comfortable bed out of my blankets and refused to move.

Just as all seemed to be lost, a ghost of a figure staggered out of the woods. It was none other than Stoddard, the man who had sold us the map in San Francisco. He was dressed in rags now, but as a crowd of haggard miners gathered round, he told a wondrous story about a lake of gold.

At this point, the reader might pause to recall that we had already been disappointed once by the stranger. Recalling that fact, the reader might further wonder why we wished to hear him out again. To that curious and thoughtful reader, I can only say, "Very good thinking."

And so we set out on the next part of our adventure.

"A lake brimming with gold, gentlemen!"
"Golden fish!"
"Nuggets the size of bird eggs"
"Fish hooks and arrowheads of gold!"
"Only a $50 guiding fee"

LAKE OF EMPTY DREAMS

IN WHICH STODDARD IS UNMASKED AND SUBJECTED TO FRONTIER JUSTICE

A s the intelligent reader may have guessed by now, Stoddard led us astray. He led 30 of us into the mountains, where winter was fast descending. We wandered in the snow until he claimed that he had lost his way. He was sure the lake of gold lay just over

FLOGGING: A COMMON PUNISHMENT FOR SMALL THEFTS; 20 LASHES IS ENOUGH TO WEAKEN A MAN TERRIBLY.

BRANDING: ONE MAN HAD THE LETTER T FOR "THIEF" BURNED INTO HIS CHEEK FOR STEALING $300 IN GOLD. (HE ALSO HAD PART OF AN EAR CUT OFF.)

this ridge or around that hillside or across yonder river. But a party of hostile Indians was the only sign of any truth in his story. After launching a few arrows—none with gold tips—they were scared off by our guns.

In the shelter of a pine grove, our party of disappointed gold seekers prepared Stoddard for his date with the system of justice common in the mining camps of California—which is to say, trial by jury of a-mob-of-angry-men-who-wish-to-see-their-prisoner-hanged-by-the-neck-until-dead. It is a system affectionately known in these parts as "Judge Lynch."

HANGING: FOR MURDER AND LARGE THEFTS.

NOTE: PUNISHMENTS IN THE MINES ARE GENERALLY ADMINISTERED NOT BY LAWMEN, WHO ARE SCARCE IN THE DIGGINGS, BUT BY ANYONE WILLING TO TAKE CHARGE.

LEDGER	Oct. 1, – Nov. 5, 1849	
BEGINNING BALANCE:		
INCOME:	$66.83	
	$0	
EXPENSES:	lost fee to Stoddard:	$50
	food:	$16*
After weeks of squirrel and scrawny deer for dinner, we nearly put Ernestine on the roasting spit.		
CURRENT BALANCE:		$0.83**
**Keep in mind, good fortune often comes when it is needed most.*		
DEBT:	$150 for Ernestine (1/3 share):	$50
	loan from Jim's uncle:	$1,000
NOTE:		

Bitter with frustration, Lansford led the angry mob. Stoddard was seized and searched. We found only $50 of the hundreds we paid him. Our party of self-appointed sheriffs named Lansford to be judge. In two hours the verdict was given and a noose prepared, but when some in our party began to argue that Stoddard should be spared so he could lead us to our money, the scoundrel slipped away into the woods.

THE RECKONING

IN A MOMENT OF SOBER REFLECTION ON OUR FORTUNES, WE DECIDE TO PART WAYS

The night after Stoddard disappeared, we all three huddled by the warmth of a fire and reflected on events of the previous months. Since May we had left our loved ones 3,000 miles away; taken three hazardous voyages upon water and three upon land; dined steadily on jerked beef, stale biscuits, and sour butter; and acquired two diseases, one stubborn donkey, and no wealth to speak of. The mountains were covered in snow. Down below the rains would soon be flooding the diggings. The time had come for us to seek our fortunes on our own.

Lansford elected to go south to the dry diggings and try one last time before returning home.

"You never said half the world had come to dig for gold, Tom."

I resolved to stay and search for gold until the flood waters swept me away.

"A man isn't a man unless he can swell his pockets with $10,000 out here."

Jim said he would return to San Francisco to make his fortune there.

"I'll have you gentlemen to tea when you come to town."

Ernestine signaled her approval of the plan that involved the least distance traveled.

MINERS AT WORK WITH LONG TOMS.

Dear Mother,

As you can see by this letter sheet, we are an industrious lot here in the diggings. Work is hard, but this is truly a land of plenty. I am in high spirits and as happy as the handsome fellow to the left of these words. I promise to send some of my earnings as soon as I am able. I hope father has found a cheap hand to help with the harvest. Tell Eva I will return with a pot of gold for us to share. Send word soon.

Yours,

Thomas

Rich Bar,
November 1849

Pity Jim and Lansford. Returning from our misadventure in the mountains, this is what I found: A claim that truly lives up to the name we bestowed upon it.

I teamed with nine other men to build a dam and waterworks, which allowed us to extract 50 ounces of gold a day from our little mountain El Dorado.

The dam clears ground for digging in the gold-laden banks of the river. It also diverts water for washing the pay dirt.

I saw a shabby figure lurking nearby and feared it might be Stoddard, though rumor has it he fled to the Oregon Territory.

Modern mining methods have not yet eliminated the need for the miner's most constant form of labor: digging dirt.

A merchant with a mule team, catching wind of our venture, has already set up shop supplying us with food. My fellow miners call him a land pirate, for he asks more than twice what we would pay in San Francisco.

LEDGER *Nov. 6, – Dec. 10,* 1849

BEGINNING BALANCE:	$0.83
INCOME: 110 lbs. of gold (1/10 share):	$2,800!!
EXPENSES: food:	$220
construction supplies:	$450
(1/10 share of lumber, nails, forged iron rods, etc.)	
donkey loan:	$150*
*In my good fortune, I could not but pay my friends' shares as well.	
CURRENT BALANCE:	$2,080!!
DEBT: loan from Jim's uncle:	$1,000

SUPPLY

Ernestine perhaps feared that our machines had eliminated the need for her services.

A common and joyous sight in our new diggings.

The wheels feed water to the Long Toms, which operate on the same principle as a cradle, only three times as fast.

A LESSON LEARNED

BEING A WARNING FOR YOUNG AND WEALTHY MINERS SET LOOSE IN THE WICKED CITY

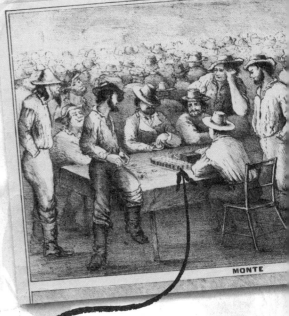

GAMBLING IN THE MIN[...]

MONTE

In December the rains came to Rich Bar and swept our dam downstream in a torrent of water. But no matter. Our claim had more than paid for our efforts. With my share secured in a purse and settled comfortably next to a new pistol at my waist, I set out to winter in San Francisco. Ernestine accompanied me willingly, proud as I to have seen industry and thrift result in our first profits from the gold fields.

However, there comes a time for every adventurer when he begins to taste the loneliness of life, when the society of friends is dearly missed and the place once filled by the gentle, civilizing influence of home and family may be taken by dark impulses. Be warned, cautious reader, that time had come for me.

As I made my way about the streets of San Francisco, flush with gold, I fell victim to the gambling establishments of Portsmouth Square, known to its denizens as the Plaza. And as I watched my hard-earned gold vanish, I longed for the companionship of my friends more than ever before.

MY LOSSES CALCULATED

MONTE: $430
UNLIKE THE RUFFIANS AT THIS TABLE, THE DEALER I OFTEN SOUGHT OUT WAS A MEMBER OF THE FAIRER SEX, A SPECIES SO RARE IN THESE PARTS THAT I FOUND MYSELF DAZZLED BY THE SIGHT.

BEAR FIGHTING: $52
MEXICANS HAVE FOR YEARS ENTERTAINED THEMSELVES BY PITTING BULLS AGAINST A CHAINED GRIZZLY BEAR. I LOST THREE OUNCES BETTING ON THE BEAR.

BILLIARDS: $244
A CURSED GAME, MADE ALL THE WORSE BY THE FACT THAT ONE MUST VISIT A SALOON TO PLAY.

DRINK: $180
MANY ESTABLISHMENTS CHARGE A PINCH OF GOLD DUST FOR A DRINK. THE MINERS CLAIM THAT BARTENDERS ARE HIRED FOR THE SIZE OF THEIR THUMBS AND FOREFINGERS.

TENPIN: $115
THIS INFERNAL GAME WAS INVENTED WHEN AUTHORITIES IN CONNECTICUT OUTLAWED NINE PINS. NOT TO BE DENIED, THE GAMBLERS SUPPOSEDLY ADDED A PIN AND CONTINUED TO PLAY.

TOTAL: $1,021

THE BELGRADE

Passage Date

Dearest Eva,

I am living well out here. Expenses are high, though thrift and quiet living can help a man make the most of his wealth. Received your letter of Nov. 15 and am happy to know you are making new friends. I cannot recall the ship captain's name, but I trust he will be leaving soon on another voyage. Did my mother purchase the little trinket for you with my earnings, as per my instructions? Tell the ship captain there is still plenty of gold to be found here and he should waste no time in coming to California.

Yours,
Tom

LEDGER	Dec. 11, '49 — Feb. 10, 1850	
BEGINNING BALANCE:		$2,080
INCOME:	loan (at 10% a month):	$300
I was forced to borrow, and lenders in California charge interest unheard of in the East.		
Lodging was scarce and food expensive as many of the city's newly constructed buildings burned to the ground		
EXPENSES:	*in Dec. 1849.* colt pistol:	$180
	2 nights, bed and board (Sacramento):	$58
	steamer passage to S.F.:	$50
	bed and board (6 weeks):	$284
	draft sent home:	$700
	gambling losses, etc.:	$1,021
CURRENT BALANCE:		$87

THE BAR OF A GAMBLING SALOON.

MARRYAT DELT.   J. BRANDARD LITH.

ALL THAT GLITTERS IS NOT GOLD

IN WHICH FAITH AND SELF-RELIANCE BEGIN THEIR RETURN

Every fortune seeker in this land of plenty must at some point scrape the bottom of their barrel and find no hope left in it. In San Francisco, sunk knee-deep in mud, I had reached that point. Yet in adversity the true adventurer finds strength.

Shelving my pride, I found what work I could. Over the next two months I unloaded cargo at the docks, chopped firewood until my hands bled, and worked as a carpenter's helper. Swearing off the gambling tables and all other forms of amusement, I began to right myself once again. As I did, my eyes opened to a wondrous sight. All around me, a new society was arising, built on a foundation of gold. And digging in the dirt was by no means the only way to make one's fortune.

In line at the post office, I met a most enterprising man. He was one William Brown, who ran an express business to and from the mines. Each weekend he delivered letters and newspapers at $1 each to men in the diggings.

Water carriers sell their precious cargo for $1 a gallon in the mines. If they're willing to make the trek, they can get five times that price from the desperate Easterners dragging themselves across the desert on the trail to the mines.

Published by T. C. BOYD, Wood Engraver, (Iron Building,) corner Washington and Montgomery sts., San Francisco.

THE CALIFORNIA WATER CARRIER.

Make a hotel from an abandoned ship and save on construction supplies.

Print letter sheets and sell them by the thousands.

I fear you'll not make your fortune selling the Word of the Lord in S.F.

HIGH AND DRY.

M. & N. HANHART IMPT

Try selling whiskey (50 cents a glass) instead of drinking it.

Lawyers, too, have made a fortune off the miners. It cost at least an ounce to have a deed drawn up for a real estate purchase. Some charge as much as $100 for a consultation. William Daingerfield, whom we met on the docks when we first arrived, made $3,300 during his first ten days as a lawyer in Sacramento.

WILLIAM DAINGERFIELD ESQ.

LEDGER *(Feb. 11 – April 10, 1850)*	
BEGINNING BALANCE:	$87
INCOME:	$128
Thanks to my poor man's diet, I was afflicted with the scurvy.	
EXPENSES: bed and board (8 weeks):	$80*
Visit to doctor:	$17
*A small slab of ground in a canvas tent and meals without vegetables	
CURRENT BALANCE:	$118
Debt increases faster than a man's dreams in California!	
DEBT: loan from Jim's uncle:	$1,000
loan from local lender (at 10% a month):	$320
NOTE:	

MAN WITH A PLAN

RELATING A TEARFUL REUNION BETWEEN TWO FRIENDS AND THE BEGINNINGS OF A PROFITABLE BUSINESS

One day, as I was unloading rolls of heavy canvas on the docks, I spied a man in fine clothes speaking earnestly to another. Imagine my astonishment when the first man turned to reveal the face of our very own Jim Bartlett.

After a long embrace, Jim told of his adventures since we parted ways. They are too numerous to recount here, but I must relate the most important details. He made his way back to San Francisco, noticing that the prices of goods became cheaper as he traveled farther from the gold fields. In San Francisco, he "rescued" a shipment of yams that had been left to rot. Making a deal with the ship captain who originally transported us to Sacramento, he hauled his load to a new town called Marysville. There he sold his supplies to miners making the final leg of their journey to the diggings. He returned with a bag full of gold, used it to purchase a load of pickaxes, shovels, and other tools, and did the same with them. After three more trips, he had a bankroll of $3,800, with which he bought his own small sailing ship. Now he was awaiting a shipment of canvas bolts.

And, he said with a broad grin, he had A PLAN. The plan—hurrah!—included me.

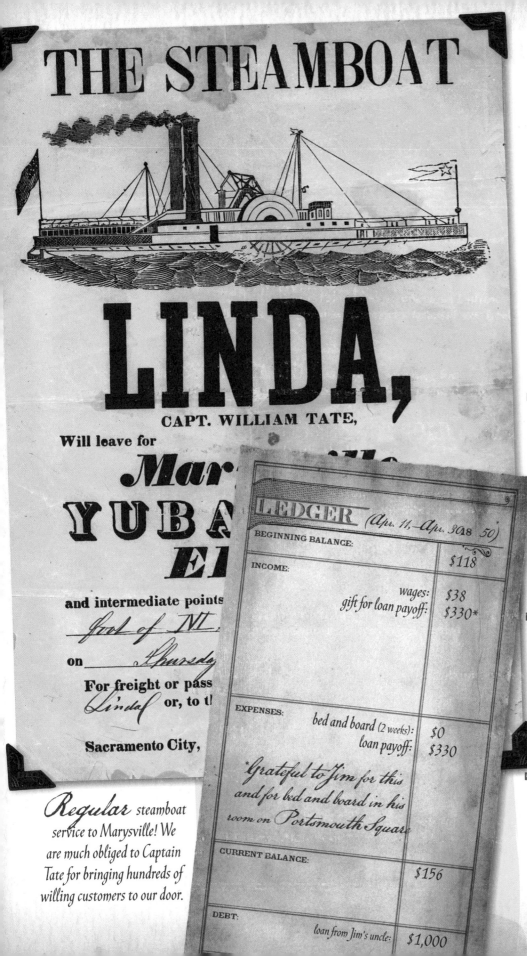

THE STEAMBOAT

LINDA,

CAPT. WILLIAM TATE,

Will leave for

Mar...ille

YUBA
EI...

and intermediate points

fork of N...

on *Thursday*

For freight or pass...
Linda or, to t...

Sacramento City,

Regular steamboat service to Marysville! We are much obliged to Captain Tate for bringing hundreds of willing customers to our door.

LEDGER (Apr. 11.–Apr. 30 1850)

BEGINNING BALANCE:	$118
INCOME:	
wages:	$38
gift for loan payoff:	$330*
EXPENSES:	
bed and board (2 weeks):	$0
loan payoff:	$330
*Grateful to Jim for this and for bed and board in his room on Portsmouth Square	
CURRENT BALANCE:	$156
DEBT:	
loan from Jim's uncle:	$1,000

THE PLAN

☞ Labor two more weeks until shipment of canvas arrives.

☞ Arrive Marysville in time for summer migration of miners back to the diggings. Buy ten lots ($250 ea.) with $1,000 paid now and the rest on credit.

☞ Build a dry goods store on one lot, a boarding house (with gambling tables and a bar) on another. (Jim's canvas will have to do for tents until we can bring frame houses up the river from San Francisco.)

☞ Hold the remaining lots until we can sell for five times the price we paid, or build homes with rooms to rent ($100 a month per lot).

☞ Purchase two more mules ($300) and hire an enterprising miner ($10 a day) to guide new arrivals to the gold fields.

Here we stock everything from pans to potatoes.
One miner told Jim he should make pants out of his
canvas as he and his fellows wear through a pair
each month. Jim told him we had enough
to do without sewing clothes as well.

MERCHA

BARTLETT & HARTLEY
DRY GOODS

LU

HORSES →

BEST
BEANS

WANTED

COFFEE

LINDA

Solid frame houses arrive regularly aboard the *Linda*. They are enough to
make an optimistic man think we will soon have a city to rival Boston.

LEDGER (May 1–Oct. 31, 1850)	
BEGINNING BALANCE: *(yours truly):*	$156
INCOME:	
board:	$8,320
room:	$4,160
tavern:	$5,200
dry goods:	$3,900
transport service:	$2,400
rent (2 lots):	$1,200
Total:	$25,180
EXPENSES:	
inventory/supplies (food, dry goods, etc.):	$4,500
labor:	$1,740
real estate:	$2,500
construction labor (3 men for 2 months):	$1,440
building frames / construction supplies:	$4,200
Total:	$14,380
CURRENT BALANCE:	$10,800
current balance (yours truly):	$5,556!!!*
DEBT: loan from Jim's uncle:	$1,000
NOTE: *Includes ½ share of profits above—grateful to Jim for this.*	

TALE OF WOE

IN WHICH LANSFORD IS DISCOVERED IN DIRE CONDITION AND RECOUNTS HIS GRIM ADVENTURES SINCE WE PARTED

THE SHAFT.
The above is a very truthful representation of

With our newfound wealth, the only sorrow that remained was the loss of our third traveling companion. In the late fall, however, Jim returned from San Francisco with a ragged ghost of a man clinging to his shoulder for support. Yes, it was Lansford suffering from exhaustion, poverty, a lung ailment, and blighted hope.

Here is his tale, as described to us over a nourishing meal of bear steak, beans, and apple pie.

In December, Lansford arrived in Stockton to find claims even more scarce than in the north and crowded with miners from Mexico, Chile, and other southern lands. Bitter and angry, our friend joined a mob of American miners, who turned out with rifles and drove the foreigners out. In the process they arrested 16 Chilenos, tried them for murder, and hanged them. The miners took over the dead men's claims and their possessions.

By the spring, Lansford wanted to return home but had not enough money to do so. He continued south to Mariposa where a new kind of mining is taking hold. He toiled for a large company deep underground, chopping quartz out of the bedrock to get the gold within. The men who do this breathe sour air and break their backs 12 hours a day. They earn $100 a month for risking their lives—if the company can afford to pay them.

40

Quartz Miners

labor in noxious dust-filled air hundreds of yards underground, a far cry from the fresh mountain air of the river claims. But alas, the lone miner with his pan and shovel may soon be a distant memory.

Finally, Lansford could take no more. He made his way to San Francisco, hoping to shovel coal on a steamship in exchange for passage home. Jim found him slumped outside a church, waiting for the soup kitchen to hand out its daily supply of free food.

HOME SWEET HOME AGAIN

ON RETURNING WITH YOUR HEAD HELD HIGH

And so the tale of my first adventures in the gold fields of California comes to a profitable end. I returned home in March 1851, exactly two years after my departure. I took with me $4,000 in profit—$1,000 for Jim's uncle, $1,500 for my family's creditors, and $1,500 as plain evidence of my becoming a man. I left the rest to be reinvested in the business. Jim stayed behind to look after the operations with Lansford, who recovered rapidly from his ailments upon reading our balance sheets.

My homecoming was joyous indeed.

My sweetheart, Eva Braintree

"Of course I will marry you, Tom Hartley. When shall we leave for California?"

"As I often say, there's nothing like a good journey to turn a young lad into a man."

My father, Elijah Hartley

"Elijah, never mind the cows. Come and meet your grown son, Thomas."

My mother, Jane Hartley

Jim's Uncle

"A fair return on a small investment, I would say. Shall we talk about a new partnership, young man?"

GOING IN TO IT.

MAKING SOMETHING.

GOING OUT OF IT.

Rey. corner of Montgomery & Commercial Sts. S.F.

LEDGER (Nov. 1, 1850 – March 15, 1851)

BEGINNING BALANCE:	$5,556
INCOME:	
Marysville profit:	$4,920
S.F. rent:	$600
EXPENSES:	
tailor:	$220
entertainment:	$760*
new property:	$3,500**
Jim's uncle:	$1,000
family debt:	$1,500
loan to Lansford:	$1,000
reinvestment:	$1,596
CURRENT BALANCE:	$1,500

*Theater and fine dining exclusively; no monte, tenpin, or billiards

DEBT:
** A building near the Plaza that has already earned two months' rent

NOTE:

A FINAL WORD

IT HAS BEEN SAID THAT THE GOLD FIELDS ARE "NATURE'S GREAT LOTTERY SCHEME." AND SO IT IS IN CALIFORNIA. IN THE DIGGINGS, MANY A MAN TOILS WITH GREAT INDUSTRY AND YET ENDS WITH NOTHING TO SHOW FOR HIS LABORS, WHILE THE NEXT MAN, THROUGH NO GREAT SKILL OF HIS OWN, GROWS RICH. FROM MY OBSERVATIONS, THE LOSERS ARE FAR MORE NUMEROUS THAN THE WINNERS. WHAT IS CERTAIN IS THAT CIVILIZATION IN THAT GLORIOUS LAND OF PLENTY WILL CONTINUE TO GROW. AND EACH NEW CITIZEN OF CALIFORNIA MUST HAVE FOOD TO EAT, TOOLS TO USE, AND A PLACE TO LAY HIS HEAD. THE PERSON WHO CAN FILL THOSE NEEDS WITH THRIFT AND IMAGINATION CAN MAKE HIS FORTUNE AFTER ALL.

Thomas Hartley

43

THOMAS HARTLEY'S GOLD RUSH

AN AFTERWORD BY MARC ARONSON

AT THE REQUEST OF National Geographic, I have carefully read this manuscript in an attempt to determine whether it is truly an authentic account of a young man's experience in the California gold rush. I confess that after consulting Dr. Peter Blodgett of the Huntington Library, an expert on the gold rush, I am still puzzled. No record of a Thomas Hartley or his friends and family has survived the years.

Aside from the fact that it is an apparent fabrication, this account of one man's sojourn in the gold fields is entirely believable. He mentions many people who certainly were part of the story of the great migration to California, including John Sutter, Rufus Porter, J. M. Hutchings, William Daingerfield, William Brown, and Mary Murphy. All the places named in the book were real. According to several accounts from the time, a shady character named Stoddard did actually lead dozens of miners on a wild-goose chase into the mountains hunting for a supposed "lake of gold." Many of the images in the book date from the 1850s or earlier and still exist today in archives and museums. As for the illustrations drawn in Hartley's hand, Stoddard's vision of Gold Lake is clearly meant as a fantasy, for there were no totem poles in California, and who could believe in a living fish made of gold? The others seem realistic, but suspect.

The adventures described in this book mirror the experience of thousands of people in the years following the gold strike at John Sutter's mill. When the news began to spread, young men flooded into California from as far away as Peru, Chile, Australia, and China. The city of San Francisco sprung up almost overnight. And that was just the start: by January 1851, 100,000 people had reached California by land and sea. Many, like Thomas and his friends, saw their fortunes rise and fall: finding a bit of gold, falling victim to crooks, losing money to gambling and drink, then—if they were resourceful—thinking up new ways to get rich. Entrepreneurs sold guidebooks to miners, housed them in hotels, or made sturdy clothing for them. These men got rich without ever looking for gold. A young man named Levi Strauss, for instance, arrived in San Francisco in the 1850s and made a fortune selling hardy denim jeans to all the new arrivals.

California during the years of the gold rush was as wild as Thomas Hartley describes. Towns like Marysville, located perfectly on the river route from Sacramento to the mines, sprung up in a matter of weeks. Jim Bartlett's enterprise sounds a lot like the experience of Stephen J. Field, a young lawyer who arrived in San Francisco in December 1849. In less than a month, he had bought 65 lots in the new town of Marysville and gotten himself elected as mayor. He made a fortune dispensing legal services and selling real estate, then went on to become a Supreme Court justice. The gold fields were also full of scam artists like Stoddard, and if these men were caught they rarely had established courts in which to plead their cases. More often they were given a hasty trial in a mining camp, then whipped, banished, or strung up on a noose hung over a tree branch.

In the gold fields, foreigners and Indians had even fewer rights than accused criminals. The lynching of Chilean miners in the southern mines described by Lansford did in fact take place in December 1849. Chinese miners, who numbered 10,000 by 1852, also got a mixed welcome. They were often kicked out of mining camps by white prospectors who were jealous of the competition. The Indians of California, who once had the entire region to themselves, probably suffered worst of all from the gold boom. Before the gold strike at Sutter's mill, about 150,000 Indians lived in California. By 1870, only 30,000 of them were left alive.

Long before then, the lone prospector panning for gold in a rushing stream had disappeared. Mining in California was taken over by big companies like the one that Lansford worked for. These companies used digging equipment and water pumps to extract hard-to-find gold from deep in the mountains. The gold rush was over. In its place was a thriving state that would one day be home to 33 million people, more than most countries in the world.

LIST OF ILLUSTRATIONS

These illustrations have been verified as historically authentic; copies can be found in museum collections and other reputable archives. Illustrations not listed here are attributed to Thomas Hartley and, while they appear to be accurate, their historical authenticity cannot be verified.

PAGE	DESCRIPTION
3	"The independent gold-hunter. . .": lithograph by Nathanial Currier, ca 1850
5	Detail from letter sheet: lithograph by Justh, Quirot & Co., ca 1851-52
6–7	"The Way They Go to California": lithograph by Nathanial Currier, ca 1849
7	"The New York Herald": text from the *Herald*, January 22, 1849; masthead appears to have been drawn by Thomas Hartley
11	"Hutchings' Panoramic Scenes.–Crossing the Plains": wood engraving by George H. Baker, ca 1854
12	Steerage ticket on the *Humbolt*: 1849
12	"Crossing the Isthmus": lithograph by Francis Samuel Marryat, 1855
13	"Map of the United States": by John M. Atwood, 1849
19	Details from "Hutchings' California Scenes.–Methods of Mining": wood engravings by Charles Christian Nahl, ca 1855; text by Thomas Hartley
20	Swaim's Panacea: patent medicine bottle label, ca 1846
21	Detail from "The Miners' Pioneer Ten Commandments of 1849": lithograph by Kurz & Allison's Art Studio, 1887
22	Daguerreotype by Joseph B. Starkweather, ca 1852
23	Daguerreotype by Joseph B. Starkweather, ca 1852
23	"California Gold Digger": lithograph by Kelloggs & Comstock, ca 1849-1852
24	Detail from "The Mining Business in Four Pictures": lithograph by Britton & Rey, ca 1852
29	Letter sheet: lithograph by Justh, Quirot & Co., ca 1851-52; text by Thomas Hartley
32	Detail from "Gambling in the Mines": lithograph by Britton & Rey, ca 1851-1902
33	"The Bar of a Gambling Saloon": lithograph by Francis Samuel Marryat, 1855
34	"The California Water Carrier": print by T. C. Boyd, ca 1870
35	"High and Dry": lithograph; illustration by Francis Samuel Marryat, 1855
37	"The Steamboat *Linda*": poster, 1850
40	Detail from letter sheet "Quartz Mining–Past and Present Illustrated": ca 1851-1860.
43	"The Mining Business in Four Pictures": lithograph by Britton & Rey, ca 1852

FURTHER READING

NONFICTION: Frontier Life, Gold Mining, and Gold Rush

Altman, Linda Jacobs. *The California Gold Rush in American History.* Enslow Publishers, 1997.
A colorful overview that includes brief sketches of historical figures.

Andrist, Ralph K. *The California Gold Rush.* American Heritage Publishing Company, 1961.
A well-written account with many archival illustrations.

Blodgett, Peter. *The Land of Golden Dreams.* University of California Press, 1999.
Although for adults, the text is not difficult to read and is accompanied by many color illustrations.

Blumberg, Rhoda. *The Great American Gold Rush.* Bradbury Press, 1989.
A valuable book by a Newbery honor book author with quotes from primary sources, facsimiles of posters, and many juicy details.

Ketchum, Liza. *Into a New Country: Eight Remarkable Women of the West.* Little, Brown, 2000.
Readable and inspiring.

Meltzer, Milton. *Gold: The True Story of Why People Search for It, Mine It, Trade It, Steal It, Mint It, Hoard It, Shape It, Wear It, Fight, and Kill for It.* Harper Collins, 1993.
Traces the story of gold through the centuries and around the world.

FICTION: Gold Rush

Cushman, Karen. *The Ballad of Lucy Whipple.* Clarion Books, 1996.
A spunky 12-year-old is dragged from her comfortable home in New England out to the rough-and-tumble world of California miners.

Fleischman, Sid. *By the Great Horn Spoon!* Little, Brown and Company, 1963.
A timeless adventure tale set in the year 1849.

Provenson, Alice. *Klondike Gold.* Simon & Schuster, 2005.
For younger readers, an informative picture book that looks at the gold rush in the remote Yukon territories in northwest Canada.

ONLINE RESOURCES

Researchers, young readers, teachers, parents, or librarians looking for colorful historical images and accurate information about the gold rush may find the following websites useful.

The Huntington Library: http://www.huntington.org/Education/GoldRush/
The online exhibition at this link is based on the book *The Land of Golden Dreams*, and readers of any age will find it useful both for easy browsing and as a starting point for further research. Click on the tab "Gold Rush Links" at bottom to find other interesting and useful online collections.

The California State Library: http//www.library.ca.gov/goldrush/
The gold rush collection at this link includes a wide range of artifacts, including period illustrations, maps, posters, and photographs.

Calisphere: http://www.calisphere.universityofcalifornia.edu/themed_collections/topics1.html
The gold rush collection accessible through Calisphere, a website run by the University of California, is drawn from museums and libraries throughout the University of California system.

ENCYCLOPEDIA OF THE GOLD RUSH
IN WHICH UNUSUAL WORDS ARE DEFINED AND ADDITIONAL INFORMATION IS OFFERED
ABOUT HISTORICAL FIGURES AND PLACES MENTIONED IN THE TEXT.

BUNGO ROBBERS: A bungo was a type of canoe used in Panama at the time of Thomas Hartley's journey. See pages 12–13.

CALIFORNIA, CA 1849: Although California was annexed by the United States after the Mexican-American War of 1848, it did not become a U.S. state until September 1850. By the time Thomas Hartley returned to Massachusetts in 1851, California's borders looked much as shown in the sketch on page 10. However, at the beginning of the gold rush, California was unincorporated

frontier land, as shown in the map at left from 1849. See page 10.

CHOLERA: An infectious bacterial disease of the small intestine, often contracted from infected water. See page 21 for a list of symptoms.

DAGUERREOTYPE: An early form of photography developed by the French artist Louis Daguerre that produced only a single print. The photographs on pages 22 and 23 are daguerreotypes. See also the entry below for *Joseph B. Starkweather*.

DYSENTERY: An infection of the intestines that is often caused by bacteria and spread by contact. See page 21 for a list of symptoms.

GOLD LAKE: There is a real place called Gold Lake, which is where Stoddard led miners, according to some accounts. Here is one grim picture of the lake: http://content.cdlib.org/ark:/13030/tf096n98s2/?query=lake%20of%20 gold&brand=calisphere. See pages 24–27 and also the entry below for *Stoddard*.

JAMES M. HUTCHINGS (1820–1902): Hutchings moved from England to the United States in 1848 and made and lost a fortune in the California gold fields. He

managed to get rich again as the publisher of *Hutchings' California Magazine*. This is a great website for anyone interested in Hutchings and his art: http://www.yosemite. ca.us/library/hutchings_california_magazine/. See page 10.

JERKED BEEF: Beef that has been first marinated in spices and then dried over a wood fire. See page 28.

LITHOGRAPH: A printed copy made from an original illustration or drawing. In the 1800s, although photography was just getting started, magazines had many illustrations. That is because skilled artists made detailed engravings in wood or stone, which could then be copied by magazines as lithographs. Many of the historical illustrations in this book are lithographs. See the *List of Illustrations* on page 44.

LONG TOM: A 10- to 20-foot trough that a team of miners would use to sift through promising soil. As a steady stream of water poured down the length of the trough, miners would shovel in soil. Small barriers in the trough would catch some of the gold, and miners would remove by hand any large rocks or stones. The fine dirt that collected at the bottom of the trough would later be panned or sifted in a rocker for gold dust. See pages 30–31.

JUDGE LYNCH: Slang reference to lynching. To lynch is to kill someone (usually by hanging) for an alleged offense, even though the suspect has not had a real trial. We are not sure where the name came from, but one possibility is Charles Lynch, who organized Virginians to capture and kill suspected Loyalists during the American Revolution. See page 27.

MARK (MARKS): The dupe of a con; a person who is easily deceived. See page 22.

MARYSVILLE: Founded in January 1850, Marysville flourished during the gold rush to become a thriving city of more than 10,000 by 1857. But Marysville's prospects dimmed with the passing of the gold rush, and, at 12,000

residents, its population today is not much changed from the 1850s. See pages 36–39.

MONTE: A game of chance, Spanish in origin, played with 40 cards (the 10s, 9s, and 8s are discarded). In two-card monte, the dealer draws a card from the top of the deck (the top layout) and another from the bottom of the deck (the bottom layout) and places both face up on the table. Players can then bet on either layout. The dealer then turns the deck over to reveal the bottom card (the gate). If the suit of the gate matches one of the layouts, the dealer pays the players' bets. If the suit of the gate card is different from either layout, the players lose their bets. In four-card monte, two top and two bottom layouts are dealt, increasing the odds for the players. See page 32.

PANACEA: A universal remedy or medicine; a cure-all. See page 20.

RUFUS PORTER (1792–1884): American artist, inventor, and founder of the *Scientific American* magazine. In an advertisement in 1849, Porter sought passengers for an "Aerial Transport" that would carry gold seekers from New York to California. Despite success with scale models, a full-size flying machine was never completed. See page 7.

RICH BAR, CALIFORNIA: A booming mining town during the gold rush. According to an account left by the wife of a Rich Bar doctor, it was also a violent place: "In the short space of 24 days, we have had several murders, fearful accidents, bloody deaths, whippings, a hanging, an attempt at suicide and a fatal duel." See page 30.

SALT PORK: Dried, salted pork, often part of a sailor or soldier's rations in the 19th century. See page 17.

SAN FRANCISCO: When gold was discovered in January 1848, San Francisco was little more than a village of 800 people. But when word of the great gold strike echoed around the world, from every corner came adventurers and prospectors. Tents were thrown up outside the town, soon to be followed by brick buildings, and almost overnight a noisy, boisterous city arose. By 1850, San Francisco had grown to 20,000 people; by 1852, 36,000; and by 1860, 50,000. In its muddy streets, immigrants from France, Germany, Mexico, China, and other nations rubbed shoulders, and its harbor was a sea of masts, as shown in the daguerreotype above from 1850. See pages 14–15.

SCURVY: A disease caused by a lack of vitamin C in the diet. See page 21 for a list of symptoms.

STODDARD (dates unknown): Stoddard's first name is listed in some sources as Robert and in others as Thomas. If you want to know more, this is a good source: http://www.sieranevadavirtualmuseum.com/docs/galleries/history/mining/goldlake.html.
See pages 14, 16, 18, 24–28, 30, 44, and also the entry above for *Gold Lake*.

JOSEPH B. STARKWEATHER (dates unknown): A successful photographer who made daguerreotypes of frontier scenes in California in the 1850s. He ran a studio in San Francisco from 1869 until possibly as late as 1899. The daguerreotypes on pages 22 and 23 were created by him. See also the entry above for *daguerreotypes*.

JOHN AUGUSTUS SUTTER (1803–1880): On January 24, 1848, contractor James Marshall discovered gold on the site of a sawmill he was building for John Sutter. Shortly thereafter, Sutter's property was overrun with prospectors. Though his name would forever be associated with the gold rush, Sutter's businesses failed and he died almost penniless. See page 6.

JOSEPH E. WARE (dates unknown): Author of the *Emigrants' Guide to California*, first published in 1849, which offered advice to travelers on the overland route to California. See page 10.

Thank you to Dr. Peter Blodgett, Curator of Western Historical Manuscripts at the Huntington Library, and Dr. Thomas Hubka, Professor of Architecture at University of Wisconsin, for guidance on matters of historical accuracy; and to Dr. Myra Zarnowski, Chair and Professor of Elementary and Early Childhood Education at Queens College, and Teri Ruyter, project director of a Teaching American History grant, for reviewing the book (and especially Thomas Hartley's bookkeeping!) with the eyes of its modern young readers.

A Book by Aronson & Glenn LLC and Tod Olson LLC
Produced by Marc Aronson, John W. Glenn, and Tod Olson
Text by Tod Olson
Book design, art direction, and production by Jon Glick, mouse+tiger
Illustrations by Scott Allred and Gregory Proch

Published by the National Geographic Society
John M. Fahey, Jr., President and Chief Executive Officer
Gilbert M. Grosvenor, Chairman of the Board
Tim T. Kelly, President, Global Media Group
Nina D. Hoffman, Executive Vice President;
    President, Book Publishing Group

Prepared by the Book Division
Nancy Laties Feresten, Vice President, Editor in Chief, Children's Books
Bea Jackson, Director of Design and Illustrations, Children's Books
Amy Shields, Executive Editor, Series, Children's Books
Jennifer Emmett, Executive Editor, Reference and Solo, Children's Books
Carl Mehler, Director of Maps

Staff for This Book
Jennifer Emmett, Project Editor
David Seager, Art Director
Lori Epstein, Illustrations Editor
Rebecca Baines, Assistant Editor
Grace Hill, Associate Managing Editor
Lewis Bassford, Production Project Manager
Jennifer A. Thornton, Managing Editor
R. Gary Colbert, Production Director
Susan Borke, Legal and Business Affairs

Manufacturing and Quality Management
Christopher A. Liedel, Chief Financial Officer
Phillip L. Schlosser, Vice President
Chris Brown, Technical Director
Nicole Elliott, Manager

Library of Congress Cataloging-in-Publication Data

Olson, Tod.
  How to get rich in the California Gold Rush : an adventurer's guide to the fabulous riches discovered in 1848 ... / Thomas Hartley ; by Tod Olson ; illustrated by Scott Allred ; afterword by Marc Aronson.
      p. cm.
  "Neither the particulars of Mr. Hartley's journey, nor in fact the existence of Mr. Hartley himself, can be verified by independent means"--Editor's note.
  Includes bibliographical references and index.
  ISBN 978-1-4263-0315-9 (trade : alk. paper) -- ISBN 978-1-4263-0316-6 (library : alk. paper)
  1. California--Gold discoveries--Juvenile literature. 2. Frontier and pioneer life--California--Juvenile literature. 3. Gold mines and mining--California--History--19th century--Juvenile literature. 4. Prospecting--California--History--19th century--Juvenile literature. 5. California--History--1846-1850--Juvenile literature. I. Allred, Scott, ill. II. Title.
  F865.O44 2008
  979.4'04--dc22

                            2008019601

ILLUSTRATION CREDITS
Abbreviations:
SA = illustration(s) by Scott Allred
JG = illustration(s) by Jon Glick, mouse+tiger
GP = illustration(s) by Gregory Proch
BL = courtesy The Bancroft Library, University of California at Berkeley
CSL = courtesy The California History Room, California State Library, Sacramento, California
HL = courtesy The Huntington Library, San Marino, California
LOC = courtesy The Library of Congress
t = top, b = bottom, c = center, l = left, r = right

Front cover (tl, c, and hand-drawn type): SA; front cover (tr): GP; front cover (background map): JG; spine (b and hand-drawn type): SA; back cover (tl, hand-drawn type, and br): SA; back cover (tc): GP; back cover (tr and bl): BL; back cover (cl and cr): CSL

Page 1 (tl and hand-drawn type): SA; page 1 (tr): GP; page 3: CSL; page 5: BL; page 6 (b, t): SA; pages 6-7 (c): BL; page 7 (t): JG; page 8 (all): GP; page 9: SA; page 10: JG; page 11: BL; page 12 (t): HL; page 12 (b): BL; page 13: LOC; pages 14-15: SA; page 16 (all): SA; page 17 (t): JG; page 17 (b): SA; page 18 (all): SA; page 19 (all): BL; page 20 (t): LOC; page 20 (b): SA; page 21 (t): CSL; page 22 (l): SA; page 22 (r): CSL; page 23 (t): CSL; page 23 (b): BL; page 24 (t): BL; pages 24-25 (c): SA; pages 26-27 (all): SA; page 28 (bl): SA; page 28 (tr): GP; page 29: BL; pages 30-31: SA; page 32 (t): BL; page 32 (b) JG; page 33 (t): JG; page 33 (b): BL; page 34 (t): SA; page 34 (b): BL; page 35 (t): BL; page 35 (b): SA; page 36: SA; page 37: CSL; pages 38-39: SA; page 40 (t): HL; page 40 (b): SA; page 41: SA; page 42 (all): GP; page 43 (t): BL; page 43 (b): SA; page 46 (l): LOC; page 46 (r): BL; page 47 (l): Public Domain; page 47 (r): LOC

Founded in 1888, the National Geographic Society is one of the largest nonprofit scientific and educational organizations in the world. It reaches more than 285 million people worldwide each month through its official journal, NATIONAL GEOGRAPHIC, and its four other magazines; the National Geographic Channel; television documentaries; radio programs; films; books; videos and DVDs; maps; and interactive media. National Geographic has funded more than 8,000 scientific research projects and supports an education program combating geographic illiteracy.

For more information, please call 1-800-NGS LINE (647-5463) or write to the following address:

National Geographic Society
1145 17th Street N.W., Washington, D.C. 20036-4688 U.S.A.

Visit us online at www.nationalgeographic.com/books

For librarians and teachers: www.ngchildrensbooks.com

More for kids from National Geographic: kids.nationalgeographic.com

For information about special discounts for bulk purchases, please contact National Geographic Books Special Sales: ngspecsales@ngs.org

For rights or permissions inquiries, please contact National Geographic Books Subsidiary Rights: ngbookrights@ngs.org

Printed in Mexico